THE YOUNG BRITISH POETS

THE YOUNG
BRITISH POETS

Edited by
JEREMY ROBSON

1971
CHATTO & WINDUS
LONDON

Published by
Chatto and Windus Ltd
42 William IV Street
London W.C.2

★

Clarke, Irwin & Co Ltd
Toronto

ISBN 0 7011 1769 9

Printed in Great Britain by
Richard Clay (The Chaucer Press) Ltd
Bungay, Suffolk

Illustrations

To
CAROLE
and for
DEBORAH &
MANUELA

Contents

Introduction

In compiling this anthology I have aimed to present a representative selection of work by the younger poets who have emerged in Britain over the past few years. None was born before 1935, and in fact most are in their middle twenties or early thirties. Apart from their youth, their only common links are the language they write in, the richly varied poetic tradition they inherited and the country they inhabit. Some are already fairly well established, with several volumes to their credit; others are not. All, however, do seem to have attained a definite measure of achievement and this (apart from the age-limit) has been my sole criterion for selection.

Poetry is now remarkably popular in Britain, and by popular I mean that a large and growing number of people listen to it, buy it, feel it to be relevant to their lives. The attendance at poetry readings, the mass sale of poetry paperbacks, the new books which flow from both the small and larger presses—all this would seem to point to some kind of renaissance. One is reminded at times of the fervour surrounding the dominant young poets of the 'thirties, though as Stephen Spender pointed out in a recent interview, the interest then was in fact restricted to 'a small circle, a clique', and his first volume, while a critical success, 'took a long time before it sold a thousand copies'. The current phenomenon is an exciting and perhaps unprecedented one, full of potential, fraught with dangers and deceptions of all kinds, especially for the poet.

The danger is that he will start writing for that audience, one eye over his shoulder and his ears straining towards anticipated applause. That this danger is real is evidenced by the current equating in some quarters of pop-song lyrics with poetry, as well as by the work of the so-called 'pop', 'sound', 'concrete', etc., poets themselves: entertaining and punny perhaps, but rarely developed to the point where it bears rereading on the page, which is where a poem—because of the complexities of its structure, music, imagery and so on—finally belongs. Certainly readings have played, and continue to play, an important role in creating an audience for the new poetry and in leading many to buy books and explore poetry on the page—justification enough. Yet at the same time it must be recognised that readings have grossly inflated the reputations of certain showmen to the detriment of some more genuine talents who have been getting on quietly with the serious business of writing the poems they had to write. It is really a question of priorities, of a commitment to poetry preceding a commitment to the media of entertainment and the world of publicity to which F. R. Leavis referred in a not too dissimilar context.

I think most of the poets represented here would see their commitment as being first and foremost to the printed word. Their work seems to me to be not only true unto itself, but to have the linguistic muscle to communicate a particular world to the general reader. This is important, for by saying poetry is not 'pop' one is not calling for poetry that is precious, remote, scholarly or abstruse. (Indeed, the mini-poems now praised in certain 'respectable' quarters are often as lamentably thin as their pop- and Beat-inspired counterparts are flabby.) Nor is one implying in any way that poetry can and should be enjoyed only by an élite—though one *is* perhaps saying that it is more valuable and responsible to aim for the highest common denominator rather than the lowest. Since poems are composed of words, and it is the way these words are used to contain a particular experience that makes a poem distinct, there can be no compromise, either to the language or the experience, which is why catchy advertising slogans thrown together for instant appeal do not make lasting poems, and why almost all the verse written about the Bomb, Vietnam and so on, in the safety of Hampstead, Liverpool or wherever, dies with the headlines it echoes.

It is against this bright and often fickle general backcloth of interest and activity that the work of the Young British Poets should be viewed. Undoubtedly the overall climate will have affected them in perhaps quite unconscious ways, just as various literary influences will have done. Yet without pointing to individuals or citing particular examples, one may contend that the most successful of the poems included are in fact craftsmanlike products, deeply rooted in personal experience, drawing their landscape and substance from individual (and sometimes regional) backgrounds and environments. It is interesting to note that these poets have not been overwhelmed by American influences as so many of their contemporaries have, and that, without being insular, they have continued to write within the English tradition.

To say more would be an intrusion. It is for the poems to speak for themselves in their varied and compelling voices.

JEREMY ROBSON

TANER BAYBARS

b. Nicosia 1936. His first book of poems (in Turkish) was published in 1953. He came to England in 1965 to study Law but never began. He adopted London as his home and English as his literary language, and now works for the British Council in their Books Division. His first collection of poems in English, *To Catch a Falling Man*, was published in 1963 and his first novel, *A Trap For the Burglar*, in 1965. In 1967, Cape published his translations (from the Turkish) of Nazim Hikmet's poems. His most recent book is a work of 'self-biography' entitled *Plucked In a Far-off Land*.

Little Paul's Moon Hut

Because this house I'm diminishing in now
is clocked and watched,
and because hands go round and round
and round without a pause,
because clocks and watches go
even if not wound,
I name the house a house, I think
it is live. Air balloons through cracks,
the sun remains caged
on the head of a nail
that juts
out from a bowed tin
majestically called a drain pipe.

But down
the hut
is watchless and clockless,
to me timeless. But there's time
within its every inch square.
Within my ticking microcosm,
dry and above such trivialities
as rhizomes, bulbs and other
inert existences,
my heart may be beating
less audibly
than the thundering silence
of that hut.

TANER BAYBARS STEWART CONN

KEITH BOSLEY

PETER DALE

KEVIN CROSSLEY-HOLLAND

DOUGLAS DUNN

Burglary

He came, took nothing, but only scraps, such as
waste-paper, half-eaten fruit and only a shoe.
What did he think seeing this picture? One book
is on the chair. He must have read. Thought what?
I see his finger-prints on the cutlery; the stove
is still hot. He must have cooked. And eaten. And
leaving, he left no dead leaf on the garden path.

He comes, takes almost everything and leaves nothing
but only scraps, such as waste paper and only a shoe.
That picture is gone and all the books. What happens
then, if he changes his mind and brings them back?
Even if not, the policy will cover the loss, nothing
was after all irreplaceable. Buy new things. Furnish
the rooms. Build a new fire. And thank God.

He will come, will take nothing that the policy covers.
Hungry to take away, he will take away what
remained unnoticed, unprofitable and I
will lose. He must not come. Although hidden,
his deft eyes may see what enemies do not,
what friends cannot think of seeing. That he must not
burgle. I shall prepare for him a marvellous trap.

B

The Long Visitors

They stayed until the floorboards
showed through the carpet. And,
what's more they had nothing to say.
As if they had left their heads behind,
and their tongues became their toes,
beating the carpet, eating. Ugly, I know.

Though, that's why the floorboards show.
Each sentence, adulterated scandal
freezes the pipes even above the hearth.
And the most eloquent of friends finds
last night's seduction the most important.
His tongue in his toes. Ugly, I know.

That's why the boards went down: one said, No.
We had been saying yes, yes, yes. Until
this gatecrasher burst and spelled the word,
made us sit down in a circle and vanish
one by one, leaving no sign, saying no
goodbye. Just vanishing, visitors and the host.

KEITH BOSLEY

b. 1937 in the Thames Valley, where he still lives. He graduated in French from Reading University in 1960 and since then has worked for the BBC External Service. His first book of poems, *The Possibility of Angels*, was published in 1969, and he has just completed a second book. His three other published books are: *Tales of the Long Lakes* (Finnish Legends), 1966; *Russia's Other Poets* (joint Editor), 1968; *An Idiom of Night* (versions from Pierre Jean Jouve).

The Old Postcards

I have often thought
of justice, of setting
my own square inch in order
of sending them back, of finding
someone to send them to
or of some simple ritual
involving water
but the old postcards of Prague
are still there in my room.
My grandfather found them
in a London street during the war
and for no good reason
took them home.
They were in a handsome album
with family photographs and the next time
he came to see us he brought the album
as a present for his small grandson.
My parents first removed the snapshots
and threw them on the fire—I could see people
curling at the edges. Laying the postcards
out on the floor I used to wonder
at so many synagogues
at tangled cemeteries with headstones
curiously inscribed, and turning them over
at captions in several languages
with German always carefully struck out.

Having since grown
a language away from my family
I offer these words
to one who may have lost the need for them.

Number 14

That house you took me to
as a child, with its steps down
from the pavement into a doorway
that smelled of damp, along a passage
into a parlour with a black-leaded grate
and a brace of partridge in white
porcelain, that house
where you grew up under your father's belt—
I pass it every day, and up till now
I have watched the street it stood in
fall to the bulldozers, house by house
each day a bit more sky:
old man, the bulldozers have gone away
and your house is still there
its red front door still saying Number 14
its windows hooded with corrugated iron
jagged against the sky; its time come
and gone, waiting for one more stroke.

Wind at Midnight

The night I was away you said the wind
vaulted the horizon, tore overland
snatched at the trees and stole their dark green sleep
fingered the river and set it gasping

and then walked to our house, quite quietly
to where you lay alone. You heard its tread
under the window: it tapped on the pane
as it passed round the corner to the door

and asked to be let in. You did not move
glad of your bed on such a night, wishing
that I were there to calm your strange unrest
with *Listen to the wind* and hold you close.

It asked again, grew wild, began to howl
knowing it seemed that you were fast within
and would not come. It threatened: you lay still.
What if it is somebody after all

but who, at midnight? Man or beast or ghost—
you could not go alone to see. You turned
over: nothing, or nobody. It sighed
and walked away, real as any man.

Tonight we are together. Listen: your
horizon, land, trees, river move. I stand
shut in my tomb or kennel at the door
real and whimpering as any wind.

STEWART CONN

b. Glasgow 1936, and now a radio drama producer with the
BBC. He was a Gregory Award winner in 1963, and his first
full collection of poems, *Stoats in the Sunlight*, was published
in 1968; it received a Scottish Arts Council poetry prize. A
number of Stewart Conn's stage plays have been performed:
The King, premiered by the Traverse Company during the
1967 Edinburgh Festival, was subsequently televised; the text
is included in *Penguin New English Dramatists 14*.

Ferret

More vicious than stoat or weasel
Because caged, kept hungry, the ferrets
Were let out only for the kill:
An alternative to sulphur and nets.

Once one, badly mauled, hid
Behind a treacle-barrel in the shed.
Throwing me back, Mathew slid
The door shut. From outside

The window, I watched. He stood
Holding an axe, with no gloves.
Then it sprang; and his sleeves
Were drenched in blood

Where the teeth had sunk. I hear
Its high-pitched squeal,
The clamp of its neat steel
Jaws. And I still remember

How the axe flashed, severing
The ferret's head,
And how its body kept battering
The barrels, long after it was dead.

Tremors

We took turns at laying
An ear on the rail—
So that we could tell
By the vibrations

When a train was coming:
Then we'd flatten ourselves
To the banks, the scorched
Vetch and hedge-parsley,

While the iron flanks
Rushed past, sending sparks
Flying. It is more and more
A matter of living

With an ear to the ground:
The tremors, when they come,
Are that much greater—
For ourselves, and others.

Nor is it any longer
A game, but a question
Of survival: each explosion
Part of a procession

There can be no stopping.
Though the end is known,
There is nothing for it
But to keep listening.

Todd

My father's white uncle became
  Arthritic and testamental in
  Lyrical stages. He held cardinal sin
Was misuse of horses, then any game

Won on the sabbath. A Clydesdale
  To him was not bells and sugar or declension
  From paddock, but primal extension
Of rock and soil. Thundered nail

Turned to sacred bolt. And each night
  In the stable he would slaver and slave
  At cracked hooves, or else save
Bowls of porridge for just the right

Beast. I remember I lied
  To him once, about oats: then I felt
  The brand of his loving tongue, the belt
Of his own horsey breath. But he died,

When the mechanised tractor came to pass.
  Now I think of him neighing to some saint
  In a simple heaven or, beyond complaint,
Leaning across a fence and munching grass.

Family Visit

i

Laying linoleum, my father spends hours
With his tape-measure,
Littering the floor
As he checks his figures, gets
The angle right; then cuts
Carefully, to the music
Of a slow logic. In despair
I conjure up a room where
A boy sits and plays with coloured bricks.

ii

My mind tugging at its traces,
I see him in more dapper days
Outside the Kibble Palace
With my grandfather, having
His snapshot taken; men firing
That year's leaves.
The Gardens are only a stone's throw
From where I live . . . but now
A younger self comes clutching at my sleeve.

iii

Or off to Innellan, singing, we would go,
Boarding the steamer at the Broomielaw
In broad summer, these boomps-a-daisy
Days, the ship's band playing in a lazy
Swell, my father steering well clear
Of the bar, mother making neat
Packets of waste-paper to carry
To the nearest basket or (more likely)
All the way back to Cranworth Street.

iv

Leaving my father at it
(He'd rather be alone) I take
My mother through the changed Botanics.
The bandstand is gone, and the great
Rain-barrels that used to rot
And overflow. Everything is neat
And plastic. And it is I who must walk
Slowly for her, past the sludge
And pocked marble of Queen Margaret Bridge.

Suicide

She could have thrown
Herself in front of a train
In her local station, and been prised off the line
By 'a little man with a bar of iron'.

Alternatives were the gas oven,
An overdose, a knife in the vein
Done in the heat of passion.
Instead she arrived alone

By plane, paid her fare
To the island and began
Walking across the stunted heather
Towards Rackwick. Where the bare

Cliffs were steepest, she stepped over.
They found her, every bone
Broken, the pelvis driven to the shoulder.
Why go to such bother

When other ways seem simpler?
How such inhuman composure?
Was she irresistibly drawn
Here or was it, like Karenin, a question

Of heaping error on error
To put an end to torture—
Begging, as she went down,
That she might be forgiven?

KEVIN CROSSLEY-HOLLAND

b. 1941. He has published translations of *Beowulf* and many of the Old English shorter poems (also available on record from Argo), and has written a number of books for children—including *The Green Children*, which won the Arts Council Prize for the best book for young children 1966–8. Both Turret Books and Academy Editions have published limited editions of some of his poems, and he hopes to publish his first full collection, *A Place of Stone*, during 1971. Kevin Crossley-Holland is currently Gregory Fellow in Poetry at the University of Leeds and Poetry Editor for Macmillan.

Marshland

This green land is almost inviolate.
Men have come, regarding it
As some commodity;
It will throw them off its outraged back.
Look at the surrendered houses,
The houseboats that will be next year's wrack.
Nothing changes.
As sure as the Black Death
Ribbed the sodden fields with graves,
And stranded churches like whales,
The marsh vapours
Rise and will drive intruders off.

Those who commune with this green land,
As their fathers did,
Intend no change, only survival.
They walk like penitents
Behind herds of lean cattle,
Salt-savaged ploughshares.
They talk of rot and marsh tares
And their horizons are dykes
Before the distant changes of the sea.
They are tight with few harvests,
Little loving;
In their damp bones they know belonging.

IAN HAMILTON

JOHN FULLER

TONY HARRISON

DOUGLAS HILL

SEAMUS HEANEY

GLYN HUGHES

Epithalamium
(for Stephen and Judy Kane)

The sun struck at you where you stood,
still separate, and braced bright bands
around you. It was momentary,
but absolute; then you moved on,
and in your train bridesmaid and page
uncompromised.

               All down the nave
the congregation, topped and tailed,
was mottled in the light stained glass
had caught, and altered, and passed on;
blotched red and yellow, blue, green, they
sneaked glances at each other, sang
together, watched the bride and groom.

Watched and identified: for one
a dream, and one a dream gone wrong,
for one never to come, and one
not even now a dream; and then,
through you, some sense renewed of all
that's possible, always being
unfulfilled.

              That hot Saturday
in June in a dormitory town,
the purpose of a pilgrimage:
we gazed at your coincidence,
that where you stood, by some good chance
light fell unstained and married you.

C

Confessional

I come once more to this terrible place;
As it was it is, each stone and each face

Unchanged, making an index of the change
In me. Everything here was arranged

Long ago; the wind, raking from the north,
Saw to that and sees to it. In the hearth

Coals glow and the ash flies early and late;
Every face is ruckled, sands corrugate;

Inland, those superstitious hawthorn trees
Strain away from the wind and heckled seas.

Yet I come. Here alone I cannot sham.
The place insists that I know who I am.

Elemental trinity—earth, air, sea—
Harshly advocate my humility:

You are bigoted, over-ambitious,
You are proud, you salute the meretricious.

Then I have altered this much with the years:
That I need more to admit my errors,

From fear, and a longing not to be blind;
So I am scoured by the unchanging wind,

And rid again of some superfluity
By that force uninterested in me.

And I can go, prepared for the possible;
Dream and bone set out from the confessional.

PETER DALE

b. Addlestone, Surrey, in 1938, and educated at Strode's School, Egham, and St. Peter's College, Oxford. He worked for some time in East Yorkshire, and now teaches at a school in Mordon. He reviews regularly for the magazine *Agenda*, and has published two books of poems, *The Storms* (1968) and *Mortal Fire* (1970).

Just Visiting

I walk awkwardly between the beds in row
trying to avoid the gauntlet of levelled eyes
like beggars that ask and envy me the ease
with which I take this tailored body through.

And you are one of these faces. At first
unseen, then recognised right down the ward.
Slight twitch of greeting because I would
n't like to wear that far a smile held fast.

You whine how much your cut hurts. You tell
me nurses forced you up to pack their wads
for sterilising, made you decorate the ward's
long walls with flowers. And you quite ill.

I'm supposed to be horrified, to sympathise.
Yet nurses have to get the dressings done,
nightly have boys to lay and drinks to down
like you to make their leaving home worth this.

Sister's periods, the old and wrinkled faces
pursed on nerve-strings to the clenched lips,
hours of obedience enough to bring collapse
on hangover, and then, cleaning up faeces.

And some of them have indolent golden hair.
Over there a woman is dying, the line
of used laughter hung in bands on the lean
bones. And what you say I cannot hear.

I shudder. If your eyes started to glaze
I should listen now, although it could not lead
again to lively talk, drinks, light to slide
about your belly, like brandy in a glass.

Such compassion couldn't turn a grey hair
auburn, nor startle your brows. But you will live again
and the living need a little love to go on.
You can speak now. I am here.

Gift of Words

That patience of yours,
standing half the morning
to watch a rose you planted bloom.

So long like that, years,
you have waited for me.
I have to watch you always.

Crescent of melon, your bare back
where blouse and jeans have come apart.
The windows between us.

Too impatient to watch your roses,
I want to lay my hands
on the equipoise of your hips.

You turn with a spray of roses,
a focus for my room—
fragrant cloud, I think you call them.

The petals will drop silently for days,
scented on these files and folders.
Sometimes I've heard them land.

There Will be Shots During the Performance

After the ads when the real film starts
you nuzzle for a kiss
disturbing me.
We are too old for this.
Fuzz of your hair
catches my eye till it smarts.

You settle my arm around you
like a stole.
A hulking German slits a captive's dress apart
from breast to hips.
Her acting husband, well-groomed still,
tries fisticuffs for the gun.

Your grip sweats into mine.
It could be life
If Hun, not starving victims
were well-groomed.

My eye still smarts.
He cannot miss,
Your body judders with the lead
(a couple dead)
and my arms could not prevent even this.

In Memory of a Hungarian Poet Murdered by the Nazis

A few in frozen woodlands shot,
some against high walls
secretly in conquered cities,
many they buried in massacre.
For years no one has known where.

A woodsman noted a marked tree;
some builder repoints a pocked wall
years later; a piece of litter
is always left in an awkward place;
a gardener curses bits of cloth
in the rich soil of a city park.

Something happens where they die.
Sons of killers assume their power;
a boy sensed something strange there
and into manhood avoids the place
till someone asking triggers answers.

Then comes a man, son of a comrade,
or friend of his son's friend:
in local maps a name to a wood;
high on a wall a wrong date hacked,
a herb flourished in a flowerbed
and the dead ask questions.

DOUGLAS DUNN

b. 1942 in Inchinnan, Renfrewshire, where he lived until 1964.
He has worked in various public and university libraries in
Britain and the United States. His first book of poems, *Terry
Street*, published in 1969, was a Poetry Book Society Choice
and won a Publication Award from the Scottish Arts Council.
Douglas Dunn is married and lives in Hull.

The Hunched

They will not leave me, the lives of other people,
I wear them near my eyes like spectacles.
The sullen magnates, hunched into chins and overcoats
In the back seats of their large cars;
The scholars, so conscientious, as if to escape
The things too real, the names too easily read,
Preferring language stuffed with difficulties;
And the children, furtive with their own parts;
The lonely glutton in the sunlit corner
Of an empty Chinese restaurant;
The coughing woman, leaning on a wall,
Her wedding ring finger in her son's cold hand,
In her back the invisible arch of death.
What makes them laugh, who lives with them?

I stooped to lace a shoe, and they all came back,
Dull, mysterious people without names or faces,
Whose lives I guess about, whose dangers tease,
And not one of them has anything at all to do with me.

The Clothes Pit

The young women are obsessed with beauty.
Their old fashioned sewing machines rattle in Terry Street.
They must keep up, they must keep up.

They wear teasing skirts and latest shoes,
Lush, impermanent coats, American cosmetics.
But they lack intellectual grooming.

In the culture of clothes and little philosophies,
They only have clothes. They do not need to be seen
Carrying a copy of *International Times*,

Or the *Liverpool Poets*, the wish to justify their looks
With things beyond themselves. They mix up colours,
And somehow they are often fat and unlovely.

They don't get high on pot, but get sick on cheap
Spanish Burgundy, or beer in rampant pubs,
And come home supported and kissed and bad-tempered.

But they have clothes, bright enough to show they dream
Of places other than this, an inarticulate paradise,
Eating exotic fowl in sunshine with courteous boys.

Three girls go down the street with the summer wind.
The litter of pop rhetoric blows down Terry Street,
Bounces past their feet, into their lives.

A Removal from Terry Street

On a squeaking cart, they push the usual stuff,
A mattress, bed ends, cups, carpets, chairs,
Four paperback westerns. Two whistling youths
In surplus U.S. Army battle-jackets
Remove their sister's goods. Her husband
Follows, carrying on his shoulders the son
Whose mischief we are glad to see removed,
And pushing, of all things, a lawnmower.
There is no grass in Terry Street. The worms
Come up cracks in concrete yards in moonlight.
That man, I wish him well. I wish him grass.

After the War

The soldiers came, brewed tea in Snoddy's field
Beside the wood from where we watched them pee
In Snoddy's stagnant pond, small boys hidden
In pines and firs. The soldiers stood or sat
Ten minutes in the field, some officers apart
With the select problems of a map. Before,
Soldiers were imagined, we were them, gunfire
In our mouths, most cunning local skirmishers;
Their sudden arrival silenced us. I lay down
On the grass and saw the blue shards of an egg
We'd broken, its warm yolk on the green grass,
And pine cones like little hand grenades.

One burst from an imaginary Browning,
A grenade well thrown by a child's arm,
And all these faces like our fathers' faces
Would fall back bleeding, trucks would burst in flames,
A blood-stained map would float on Snoddy's pond.
Our ambush made the soldiers laugh, and some
Made booming noises from behind real rifles
As we ran among them begging for badges,
Our plimsolls on the fallen may-blossom
Like boots on the faces of dead children.
But one of us had left. I saw him go
Out through the gate, I heard him on the road
Running to his mother's house. They lived alone,
Behind a hedge round an untended garden
Filled with broken toys, abrasive loss;
A swing that creaked, a rusted bicycle.
He went inside just as the convoy passed.

A Dream of Judgement

Posterity, thy name is Samuel Johnson.
You sit on a velvet cushion on a varnished throne
Shaking your head sideways, saying No,
Definitely no, to all the books held up to you.
Licking your boots is a small Scotsman
Who looks like Boswell, but is really me.
You go on saying No, quite definitely no,
Adjusting the small volume of Horace
Under your wig and spitting in anger
At the portrait of Blake Swift is holding up.
Quite gently, Pope ushers me out into the hell
Of forgotten books. Nearby, teasingly,
In the dustless heaven of the classics,
There is singing of morals in Latin and Greek.

JOHN FULLER

b. 1937. He won the Newdigate Prize for Poetry at Oxford University in 1960, and an E. C. Gregory Award in 1965. He is married with three children and lives in Oxford. He has lately been writing songs and libretti for the composer Bryan Kelly. He has published two books of poems, *Fairground Music* (1961) and *The Tree That Walked* (1967), the latter being a Poetry Book Society Choice. He has also written a study of W. H. Auden's poetry.

Pictures from a '48 De Soto

1

Humped in this swart sedan, paper half-lowered,
The automatic at my side snug as a cancer,
I watch the house. Or in the house myself

Look at my wrist, insane with jealousy:
Her furs and veils lie on the front seat,
The tongue inside its curious second home.

Even banked high in snow, the engine dead,
The woven greenish braids and tassels swing,
A razored head lurches, lolls back, headlights

Shattered in the pursued and silent mirror.
The windows are shut: palms thud wildly on
The glass. Black opening mouth, the sound switched off.

2

The last owner lugged gravel, the wings
Rusted and bolted back. We drive it
Three thousand miles to the Pacific

Where the blind nude hulk, down to its canvas,
Like a slow fist hisses into the dump.
Now the yellow plates illegally decorate

The bathroom, and these, too, fetch improbable ghosts:
After days on the anvil, tanking through the dust,
We arrive at the coloured river. Our eyes hurt.

Dwarfs wrestle behind glass. Dresses
Are cut to the buttocks' cleft. Half-shaved men
Are running sheeted through the empty square.

Peasant Woman: Rhodes

These are my scarves and veils and boots of sweat.
My hands are horny with the donkey's straps.
I have not borne a living baby yet:
The one inside me may be strong perhaps.
In all this heat I wear thick wool. Beneath,
At least one slip I do not often change.
And if I smile I show my metal teeth,
But I must smile because you are so strange!
You smile back too. You came to have a look
And show your photos when you end your trip.
You seem to live by writing in a book.
We live off what we get from this dry land.
You understand, and leave a decent tip
But here, you see, we do not understand.

D

Scenario for a Walk-On Part

The borrowed walking-stick that makes me lame,
The single curiously worn-down tyre,
The hanging button and forgotten name,
The grinning of the vulnerable liar:
These are the gambits of a chosen game,
A well-cut personality on hire,
Mirrors too low, the eyebrows graze the frame,
Warming my hands before an unlit fire.

Dinner a skirmish, legs uncrossed and crossed,
An alp of linen and the sight of nylons,
Pudding arriving full of fruit and frost,
And, swimming in their syrup, smoking islands,
Lips at a silver spoon proclaim me lost,
My single joke counters a threat of violence.
The table cleared, I cannot count the cost
Of dinner or of nerves. The rest is silence.

Now in the sharpest lock at close of day,
Hands as if manacled, the gravel spurting,
My hosts with linked arms waving me away,
The gulf of what I didn't say still hurting
(Since you are only known by what you say),
Yawning beneath my silent murmur skirting
The dangerous excuse, the wish to stay,
Like the evasions of protracted flirting:

Alone I drive away with my awareness
That once again I've failed the magic word
Whose demon locks me up inside my bareness,
The charming openness unsaid, unheard.
Is love the better for its hurts and rareness?
I frown and think so. Falling into third
On a hill, I glimpse a face: the sheer unfairness
Fights with my sense of shame at being stirred.

The sexy minister reclaims his scarf,
A girl in denim runs to meet a train,
Mrs Jocasta bastes the fatted calf,
The guests have taken to their beds again:
I hold the floor but nobody will laugh,
No one is there to kiss if I complain,
I enter only in the second half,
Unwilling, underwritten, used to pain.

Song

You don't listen to what I say.
When I lean towards you in the car
You simply smile and turn away.

It's been like this most of the day,
Sitting and sipping, bar after bar.
You don't listen to what I say.

You squeeze a lemon from a tray,
And if you guess how dear you are
You simply smile and turn away.

Beyond the hairline of the bay
The steamers call that shore is far.
You don't listen to what I say:

Surely there's another way?
The waiter brings a small guitar.
You simply smile and turn away.

Sometimes I think you are too gay,
Smiling and smiling, hour after hour.
You don't listen to what I say.
You simply smile and turn away.

IAN HAMILTON

b. Kings Lynn, Norfolk, 1938, and educated at Darlington Grammar School and Keble College, Oxford. Winner of the 1963 E. C. Gregory Award for poetry. He has edited three books: *The Modern Poet*, *The Poetry of War 1939–45* and *Alun Lewis: Selected Poetry and Prose*. In 1964 he published a pamphlet of poems, *Pretending Not to Sleep*, and in 1970 his first complete book, *The Visit*. He is editor of *The Review* and assistant editor of *The Times Literary Supplement*.

Pretending Not to Sleep

The waiting rooms are full of 'characters'
Pretending not to sleep.
Your eyes are open
But you're far away,
At home, *am Rhein*, with mother and the cats.
Your hair grazes my wrist.
My cold hand surprises you.

The porters yawn against the slot-machines
And watch contentedly; they know I've lost.
The last train
Is simmering outside, and overhead
Steam flowers in the station rafters.
Soft flecks of soot begin to settle
On your suddenly outstretched palms.
Your mouth is dry, excited, going home.

The velvet curtains,
Father dead, the road up to the village,
Your hands tightening in the thick fur
Of your mother's Persian, your dreams
Moving through Belgium now, full of your trip.

Trucks

At four, a line of trucks. Their light
Slops in and spreads across the ceiling,
Gleams, and goes. Aching, you turn back
From the wall and your hands reach out
Over me. They are caught
In the last beam and, pale,
They fly there now. You're taking off, you say,
And won't be back.
                              Your shadows soar.
My hands, they can merely touch down
On your shoulders and wait. Very soon
The trucks will be gone. Bitter, you will turn
Back again. We will join our cold hands together.

The Recruits

'Nothing moves' you say, and stare across the lawn
At the trees, loafing in queues, their leaves rigid;
At the flowers, edgy, poised. You turn and cry;
'The sun is everywhere. There will be no breeze.'

Birds line the gutters, and from our window
We see cats file across five gardens
To the shade and stand there, tense and sullen,
Watching the sky. You cry again: 'They know'.

The dead flies pile up on the window sill.
You scoop them into heaps. You weep on them.
You shudder as the silence darkens, till
It's perfect night in you. And then you scream.

Last Illness

Entranced, you turn again and over there
It is white also. Rectangular white lawns
For miles, white walls between them. Snow.
You close your eyes. The terrible changes.

White movements in one corner of your room.
Between your hands, the flowers of your quilt
Are stormed. Dark shadows smudge
Their faded, impossible colours
But do not settle.

You hear the ice take hold. Along the street
The yellowed drifts, cleansed by a minute's fall,
Wait to be fouled again. Your final breath
Is in the air, pure white, and moving fast.

TONY HARRISON

b. Leeds 1937 and educated at Leeds Grammar School and the University of Leeds, where he read Classics and edited *Poetry and Audience*. He lectured for four years in West Africa and one year in Prague before returning to England to become the first Northern Arts Fellow in Poetry at the Universities of Newcastle-upon-Tyne and Durham (1967–8). In 1969 he was awarded a UNESCO fellowship in poetry; he has travelled extensively in the Soviet Union, Cuba and South America. His first book of poems, *The Loiners*, was published in 1970. He now lives in Newcastle.

Thomas Campey and the Copernican System

The other day all thirty shillings' worth
Of painfully collected waste was blown
Off the heavy handcart high above the earth,
And scattered paper whirled around the town.

The earth turns round to face the sun in March,
he said, resigned, *it's bound to cause a breeze*.
Familiar last straws. His back's strained arch
Questioned the stiff balance of his knees.

Thomas Campey, who, in each demolished home,
Cherished a Gibbon with a gilt-worked spine,
Spengler and Mommsen, and a huge, black tome
With Latin titles for his own decline:

Tabes dorsalis; veins like flex, like fused
And knotted flex, with a cart on the cobbled road,
He drags for life old clothing, used
Lectern bibles and cracked Copeland Spode,

Marie Corelli, Ouida and Hall Caine
And texts from Patience Strong in tortoise frames.
And every pound of this dead weight is pain
To Thomas Campey (Books) who often dreams

Of angels in white crinolines all dressed
To kill, of God as Queen Victoria who grabs
Him by the scruff and shoves his body pressed
Quite straight again under St Anne's slabs.

And round Victoria Regina the Most High
Swathed in luminous smokes like factories,
These angels serried in a dark, Leeds sky
Chanting *Angina-a, Angina Pectoris.*

Keen winter is the worst time for his back,
Squeezed lungs and damaged heart; just one
More sharp turn of the earth, those knees will crack
And he will turn his warped spine on the sun.

Leeds! Offer thanks to that Imperial Host
Squat on its thrones of Ormus and of Ind,
For bringing Thomas from his world of dust
To dust, and leisure of the simplest kind.

A Proper Caution

The sun's in cloud. The fat man with string-vest
Patterns sun-printed on his woman's chest,
Starts up from his deck chair suddenly,
And dragging his toe-ends in the ebbing sea,
Crowned with a useless *Kiss Me*, King Canute,
Red-conked and ludicrous, but still a man,
Shouts out before the cuddlesome and cute
To death and darkness: *Stop!* to prove they ran.

Durham

'St. Cuthbert's shrine founded 999'
(*Mnemonic*)

ANARCHY and GROW YOUR OWN
whitewashed onto crumbling stone
fades in the drizzle. There's a man
handcuffed to warders in a black sedan.
A butcher dumps a sodden sack
of sheep pelts off his bloodied back,
then hangs the morning's killing out,
cup-cum-muzzle on each snout.

I've watched where this 'distinguished see'
takes off into infinity,
among transistor antennae,
and student smokers getting high,
and visiting Norwegian choirs
in raptures over Durham's spires,
lifers, rapists, thieves, ant-size,
circle and circle at their exercise.

And Quasimodo's bird's-eye view
of big wigs and their retinue,
a five car Rolls Royce motorcade
of judgement draped in Town Hall braid,
I've watched the golden maces sweep
from courtroom to the Castle keep,
through winding Durham, the elect
before whom ids must genuflect.

But some stay standing and at one
God's irritating carillon
brings you to me; I feel like the hunch-
back taking you for lunch;
then bed. All afternoon two church-
high helicopters search
for escapes down by the Wear
and seem as though they're coming here.

Listen! Their choppers guillotine
all the enemies there've ever been
of Church and State, including me,
for taking this small liberty.
Liberal, lover, communist,
Czechoslovakia, Cuba, grist,
grist for the power-driven mill
weltering in overkill.

And England? Quiet Durham? Threat
smokes off our lives like steam off wet
subsidences when summer rain
drenches the workings. You complain
that the machinery of sudden death,
Fascism, the hot bad breath
of Powers down small countries' necks
shouldn't interfere with sex.

They *are* sex, dear, we must include
all these in love's beatitude.
Bad weather and the public mess
drive us to private tenderness,
though I wonder if together we,
alone two hours, can ever be
love's anti-bodies in the sick,
sick body politic.

At best we're medieval masons, skilled
but anonymous within our guild,
at worst defendants hooded in a car
charged with something sinister.
On the *status quo*'s huge edifice
we're just excrescences that kiss,
cathedral gargoyles that obtrude
their acts of 'moral turpitude'.

But turpitude still keeps me warm
in foul weather as I head for home
down New Elvet, through the town,
past the butcher closing down,
hearing the belfrey jumble time
out over Durham. As I climb
rain blankets the pithills, mist
the chalkings of the anarchist.

I wait for the six-five Plymouth train
glowering at Durham. First rain,
then hail, like teeth spit from a skull,
then fog obliterate it. As we pull
out of the station through the dusk and fog,
there, lighting up, is Durham, dog
chasing its own cropped tail,
University, Cathedral, Gaol.

The Nuptial Torches

These human victims, chained and burning at the stake, were the blazing torches which lighted the monarch to his nuptial couch—J. L. Motley, *The Rise of the Dutch Republic*.

Fish gnaw the Flushing capons, hauled from fleeced
Lutheran Holland, for tomorrow's feast.
The Netherlandish lengths, the Dutch heirlooms,
That might have graced my movements and my groom's
Fade on the fat sea's bellies where they hung
Like cover-sluts. Flesh, wet linen wrung
Bone dry in a washerwoman's raw, red,
Twisting hands, bed-clothes off a lovers' bed,
Falls off the chains. At Valladolid
It fell, flesh crumpled like a coverlid.

Young Carlos de Sessa stripped was good
For a girl to look at and he spat like wood
Green from the orchards for the cooking pots.
Flames ravelled up his flesh into dry knots
And he cried at the King: *How can you stare
On such agonies and not turn a hair?*
The King was cool: My friend, *I'd drag the logs
Out to the stake for my own son, let dogs
Get at his testes for his sins; auto-da-fés
Owe no paternity to evil ways.*
Cabrera leans against the throne, guffaws
And jots down to the Court's applause
Yet another of the King's *bon mots*.
O yellow piddle in fresh fallen snow—
Dogs on the Guadarramas . . . dogs. Their souls
splut through their pores like porridge holes.
They wear their skins like cast-offs. Their skin grows
Puckered round the knees like rumpled hose.

Doctor Ponce de la Fuente, you,
Whose gaudy, straw-stuffed effigy in lieu
Of members hacked up in the prison, burns
Here now, one sacking arm drops off, one turns
A stubble finger and your skull still croons
Lascivious catches and indecent tunes;
And croaks: *Ashes to ashes, dust to dust.*
Pray God be with you in your lust.
And God immediately is, but such a one
Whose skin stinks like a herring in the sun,
Huge from confinement in a filthy gaol,
Crushing the hooping on my farthingale.

O Holy Mother, Holy Mother, Ho—
ly Mother Church, whose melodious, low
Labour-moans go through me as you bear
These pitch-stained children to the upper air,
Let them lie still tonight, no crowding smoke
Condensing back to men float in and poke
Their charcoaled fingers at our bed, and let
Me be his pleasure, though Philip sweat
At his rhythms and use those hateful tricks
They say he feels like after heretics.

O Let the King be gentle and not loom
Like Torquemada in the torture room,
Those wiry Spanish hairs, these nuptial nights,
Crackling like lit tapers in his tights,
His seed like water spluttered off hot stone.
Maria, whose dark eyes very like my own
Shine on such consummations, Maria bless
My Philip just this once with gentleness.

The King's cool knuckles on my smoky hair!

Mare Mediterraneum, la mer, la mer
That almost got him in your gorge with sides
Of feastmeats, you must flush this sacred bride's
Uterus with scouring salt. O cure and cool
The scorching birthmarks of his branding-tool.

Sweat chills my small breasts and limp hands.

They curled like foetuses, *maman*, and cried.

His crusted tunics crumple as he stands:

Come, Isabella. God is satisfied.

E

SEAMUS HEANEY

b. 1939, and brought up on a farm in County Derry, Ireland. He was educated at St. Columb's, Londonderry, and at Queen's University, Belfast. He has taught in a secondary school, a training college, at Queen's University, and is currently teaching at Berkeley College, California. His first collection of poems, *Death of a Naturalist* (1966), was awarded the Somerset Maugham Award, and his second, *Door into the Dark* (1969), was the Poetry Book Society Choice.

Follower

My father worked with a horse-plough,
His shoulders globed like a full sail strung
Between the shafts and the furrow.
The horses strained at his clicking tongue.

An expert. He would set the wing
And fit the bright steel-pointed sock.
The sod rolled over without breaking.
At the headrig, with a single-pluck

Of reins, the sweating team turned round
And back into the land. His eye
Narrowed and angled at the ground,
Mapping the furrow exactly.

I stumbled in his hob-nailed wake,
Fell sometimes on the polished sod;
Sometimes he rode me on his back
Dipping and rising to his plod.

I wanted to grow up and plough,
To close one eye, stiffen my arm,
All I ever did was follow
In his broad shadow round the farm.

I was a nuisance, tripping, falling,
Yapping always. But today
It is my father who keeps stumbling
Behind me, and will not go away.

The Outlaw

Kelly's kept an unlicensed bull, well away
From the road: you risked fine but had to pay

The normal fee if cows were serviced there.
Once I dragged a nervous Friesian on a tether

Down a lane of alder, shaggy with catkin,
Down to the shed the bull was kept in.

I gave Old Kelly the clammy silver, though why
I could not guess. He grunted a curt 'Go by

Get up on that gate'. And from my lofty station
I watched the business-like conception.

The door, unbolted, whacked back against the wall.
The illegal sire fumbled from his stall

Unhurried as an old steam engine shunting.
He circled, snored and nosed. No hectic panting,

Just the unfussy ease of a good tradesman;
Then an awkward, unexpected jump, and

His knobbled forelegs straddling her flank,
He slammed life home, impassive as a tank,

Dropping off like a tipped-up load of sand.
'She'll do', said Kelly and tapped his ash-plant

Across her hindquarters. 'If not, bring her back.'
I walked ahead of her, the rope now slack.

While Kelly whooped and prodded his outlaw
Who, in his own time, resumed the dark, the straw.

The Peninsula

When you have nothing more to say, just drive
For a day all round the peninsula.
The sky is tall as over a runway,
The land without marks so you will not arrive

But pass through, though always skirting landfall.
At dusk, horizons drink down sea and hill
The ploughed field swallows the whitewashed gable
and you're in the dark again. Now recall

The glazed foreshore and silhouetted log,
That rock where breakers shredded into rags,
The leggy birds stilted on their own legs,
Islands riding themselves out into the fog

And drive back home, still with nothing to say
Except that now you will uncode all landscapes
By this: things founded clean on their own shapes,
Water and ground in their extremity.

Shore Woman

Man to the hills, woman to the shore. (Gaelic proverb.)

I have crossed the dunes with their whistling bent
Where dry loose sand was riddling round the air
And I'm walking the firm margin. White pocks
Of cockle, blanched roofs of clam and oyster
Hoard the moonlight, woven and unwoven
Off the bay. A pale sud at the far rocks
Come and goes.
                Out there he put me through it.
Under boards the mackerel slapped to death
Yet still we took them in at every cast,
Stiff flails of cold convulsed with their first breath.
My line plumbed certainly the undertow,
Loaded against me once I went to draw
And flashed and fattened up towards the light.
He was all business in the stern. I called
'This is so easy that it's hardly right,'
But he unhooked and coped with frantic fish
Without speaking. Then suddenly it lulled,
We'd crossed where they were running, the line rose
Like a let-down and I was conscious
How far we'd drifted out beyond the head.
'Count them up at your end,' was all he said
Before I saw the porpoises' thick backs
Cartwheeling like the flywheels of the tide,
Soapy and shining. To have seen a hill
Splitting the water could not have numbed me more
Then the close irruption of that school,
Tight viscous muscle, hooped from tail to snout,
Each one revealed complete as it bowled out
And under.
           They will attack a boat.
I knew it and I asked John to put in
But he would not, declared it was a yarn

My people had been fooled by far too long
And he would prove it now and settle it.
Maybe he shrank when those thick slimy backs
Propelled towards us: I lay and screamed
Under splashed brine in an open rocking boat
Feeling each dunt and slither through the timber,
Sick at their huge pleasures in the water.

I sometimes walk this strand for thanksgiving
Or maybe it's to get away from him
Skittering his spit across the stove. Here
Is the taste of safety, the shelving sand
Harbours no worse than razor shell or crab—
Though my father recalls carcasses of whales
Collapsed and gasping, right up to the dunes.
But tonight such moving, sinewed dreams lie out
In darker fathoms far beyond the head.
Astray upon a debris of scrubbed shells
Between perched dunes and salivating wave,
I claim rights on this fallow avenue,
A membrane between moonlight and my shadow.

The Given Note

On the most westerly Blasket
In a dry-stone hut
He got this air out of the night.

Strange noises were heard
By others who followed, bits of a tune
Coming in on loud weather

Though nothing like melody.
He blamed their fingers and ear
As unpractised, their fiddling easy

For he had gone alone into the Island
And brought back the whole thing.
The house throbbed like his full violin.

So whether he calls it spirit music
Or not, I don't care. He took it
Out of wind off mid-Atlantic.

Still he maintains, from nowhere.
It comes off the bow gravely,
Rephrases itself into the air.

DOUGLAS HILL

b. Canada 1935, and resident in Britain since 1959. He has
been a full-time freelance writer since 1964, working in the
fields of folklore, history and literature. Author of *The
Supernatural* (with Pat Williams), *The Opening of the Canadian
West* and books on such other subjects as John Keats, Regency
London and the exploration of the USA. His poems, reviews
and articles have appeared in many British and North
American periodicals. Recipient of a Canada Council short-
term grant for poetry in 1968, he is now preparing for publica-
tion his first collection of poems, *Tourist At Large*.

Sarcophagi in the British Museum

One of this temple's galleries
is echoing with death.
Dry brown bags of human skin

scraped from the anonymous
Egyptian sand lie mortified,
exposed. Sure of our disbelief

in *ba*-souls, or their afterlife
lost if the tombs are plundered,
we have caused their cadavers to die

twice. Like Thomas Browne, who feared
exhumation as we fear burial alive
yet whom some curator pried

from his tight grave, to flaunt
his skull in a glass museum case
where it must have screamed for years.

So these husks scream, in an obscene
archaeological peep-show
and the ancient curse on desecrators

falls impotent now as the flesh
flaking on their wrinkled loins
mortified, exposed.

In Bed-Sitting Rooms

In bed-sitting rooms

love and houseplants
wither, even in April

among smells of carpet dust
dry bread and unnatural gas

the leaves fade to yellow
petals fall within hours

and outside the birds are crying
repetitive, unmusical

and the spring sun is always
shining somewhere else

while in the walled motionless
bed-sitting world

it is October between my love and me

Alpes-Maritimes

(for Hélène)

Among mountains I slide
into poetry like a loosened
slab of pink or ochre shale
tobogganing down its own avenue
of gravel. A noisy descent
an avalanche into the Romantic
echoing with Wordsworthian overhangs
above some God-lit valley.

Better that than littering
rock faces with the bootmarks
of climbers, who call it scaling
as if their ropes and pitons
scaled down the heights
to a less inhuman size.
No, I scramble among foothills
an audience exalted by tableaux
by skylines, by the stately
imperceptible geologic dance
silent till I precipitate
my small cascade of poetry or shale.

Lighthearted Myth-Song

I wear high boots to go out in the garden
And tight rubber gloves
  (sing to the marigolds)
Point my umbrella in all directions
In case it rains earth
  (sing to the concrete marigolds)

I take my dark glasses out in the garden
To soften the sky
  (laugh at the bluejays)
Handle a parasol, shoulder a shade
Draw the sun's limits
  (laugh at the concrete bluejays)

I button my collar when out in the garden
Keep my lips closed
  (dance on the pathways)
Pass unperturbed by the goat-hairs caught
On the plum tree thorn
  (dance alone on the concrete pathways)

A. C. JACOBS

BRIAN JONES

ANGELA LANGFIELD

DEREK MAHON

MICHAEL LONGLEY

DOM MORAES

GLYN HUGHES

b. 1935, and brought up in Altrincham, Cheshire. He was educated at the Grammar School there, and later at the Regional College of Art, Manchester and at Manchester University. He won the Welsh Arts Council's Young Poets' Prize for 1969, and his first book, *Neighbours*, published in 1970, was the Poetry Book Society Recommendation. He teaches at the High School of Art, Manchester.

Shortening Days

Moors are the still
beasts reconciled
to dying, or already dead;
that wallow in fog
of cloud-stack, collapsed
between ridges of land
hard as herring skeleton.
No breeze knocks
at these decaying days
hugged by a grey
phlegm—the yellow eye
of a field gleams and goes;
the shepherd enclosed in slow
work slurs to his hearth.

Sheep

Silently they find their tracks'
stretched wires between rushes and maced thistles,
flow after each other over broken walls
and seem boneless, like caterpillars;

become the grey liquid of mist
or are monster-sized and still on a crest
of the hills they haunt,
staring in line like Hollywood Indians;

indifferent to creatures that live on sheep,
magpies that rake their backs for wickies
and beetles that render them, when they are dead,
to a turd of skin and wool

moulded on rock after snow
and stretched by thaw-water; men
who mark them red or blue upon the flank—
indifferent to, but in on every secret.

Coming home drunk at one a.m.
with exploding breath,
the lights below a golden sand
lost to a dark sea as switches are pressed

I find that sheep are staring spectators
on the roof of the lean-to, with the ladders;
and when I wake in the morning and find
that the roses have vanished,

eaten by horned and black-masked devils
I understand why the gardeners grow only
foxgloves that are poisonous to sheep
crossed with mountain goats.

Spawning and nibbling, the Ram is the Big Dick.
Those fish that nibble a man to the bone
whilst he swims, have nothing on him.
He stares with little eyes across the moors.

The Letter

My Love returns on Saturday.
The postman who doesn't stay
one minute, sees me part the paper:
seven years married, I ought to know better
than let my hands shake on the lips of her letter.

Three cumbersome days, before that date,
for eating and for drinking, for trying to write
poems, for me to lumber through
anyway I can! Those days should know
three more letters from you.

What if they don't come?
Carefully I store this too meagre one
on the mantelpiece, noticing
Yeats on the Irish stamp, and your handwriting
sprawled the way you lie sometimes, inviting.

In windows I see myself, my thin
hair blown to show my skull and skin
as I walk the town and look for women like her
with brown eyes, no make-up, darkened hair
and looking ten years younger than they are,

to wonder if another could take her place.
I find it in no face.
I only think of her words as I walk the street:
'We are a unity that cannot be split'
she wrote: 'Our trouble cannot be made separate'.

I know how I will meet her from the bus,
spilling my love. Back at the house
'Don't be silly' she will say, 'Don't fuss'.

A. C. JACOBS

b. Glasgow 1937 and educated at local state schools there, and later at a Jewish grammar school in London. He now lives in London, but has lived in Israel, Italy and in remote parts of Scotland. He has done many translations from Hebrew poetry, some of which have appeared in relevant anthologies.

Travelling Abroad

Documents, scrutinies, barriers,
Everywhere I pass through them,
It seems, without difficulty.
Nothing jars, nothing slips out of place,
Authority is satisfied by my credentials.

Really, it must represent some peak
Of achievement, from a Jewish
Point of view, that is.
                              What a time
It's taken to bring me
To this sort of freedom,
What tolls have been paid
To let me come
                    to this kind
Of passage.

I can appreciate it,
                    believe me,
I can appreciate.

              .

But I find myself wondering,
As I sit at this café table
                              over
A good glass of beer,
Why I don't feel something more
                                        like gratitude,
Why there's some form of acceptance
I don't grasp.

Lines

I wrote some lines describing you
As though I had brought
                              a kind of clarity
To bear on your experience,
As though something, in verse,
Of what you cannot say
                              was made
Articulate.
                    It is a helplessness
Of my own that stares up from the page.
The phrases that were meant
To draw and plead for you
Only dissect,
                    make you more a stranger,
Trap.
         Not everything
                              is grist for poetry,
Not observation
                    made in place of care.

Remote Island

There was that lonely island in the North,
Best for the birds, but a few people lived there
In small and difficult crofts.
                              There was a hill
That rose slowly, on one side of it, and across the top
Were the ruins of a war-time establishment.
                                        Huge
Water-tanks rusted there, and tough generators
Lay in derelict silence, crumbling.
                                Strong walls had just
A few gaps in them, but broken fences swayed over
The hillside.
            It was like the remains
Of a previous civilisation on the island,
Though it was twenty years or so ago, the place
Was built.
            And strolling through it, you could see
How expertly the war had raised it up,
And just as quickly had dismantled it,

Leaving the island, still depopulated,
In its old remoteness, at the edge of things.

Festa

Today they say was the feast
Of *Corpus Domini*
                    And coming round
By the cathedral, I blundered
Into the vast crowds gathered
To watch the spectacle.
                        There were
Slow drum taps, and then the
Banners came, swaying out of
The great doors, and round the square,
Followed by God's agony carved
On a little cross of sticks.
                            An anthem
Struck up through the well-placed
Loudspeakers, and someone prayed
In a level, finely pitched voice
For the poor, the prisoners, the sick
And unemployed.
                    The crowd answered
Ascoltaci,
            and a white canopy
Like a *chuppah* came billowing round.

I saw many near me duck and
Cross themselves in their devotion.
                                It was
Soaring and death, on the square
Of San Giovanni, a glimpse at a
Beautiful ceremony.
                    I lit a cigarette,
Thoughtfully, and walked away.

BRIAN JONES

b. 1938. He is married with two children, works as a teacher and lives in Canterbury. He has published three books of poems, *Poems* (1964), *A Family Album* (1968) and *Interiors* (1969). He was the subject of a recent television documentary.

Local Custom

The cranes along this sea-coast
Swing inward often away from dust and brick
And the bitter North Sea towards the hills
Two miles off. When they do, you know
That a couple on the slopes are making love,
Spotted and relished through binoculars.
Work stops. Men on the sites below
Jeer upwards, squat on rubbish, swap sex-stories,
While remote crane-drivers sway in their lucky cabs
And keep the glasses steady. What is there to do
When those graceful arms make such an indication?
You look up from your spade, your shopping list,
Your car, your tennis-racket, your prize-rose,
Towards those hills where the sea-wind smacks your head,
Would rip off rose-petals, bedevil the cunningest lob,
And chuck polite words over the hills' shoulder.
Until those cranes, with somewhat regretful pace,
Turn back to rubble, you can only wait
Irritably, scratch your nose or groin,
Sigh, look skyward, beat out a flippant tune,
And wait until significance resumes
Its mild disguise—rose, Jaguar, or ball.

Husband to Wife: Party Going

Turn where the stairs bend
In this other house; statued in other light,
Allow the host to ease you from your coat.
Stand where the stairs bend,
A formal distance from me, then descend
With delicacy conscious but not false
And take my arm, as if I were someone else.

Tonight, in a strange room
We will be strangers: let our eyes be blind
To all our customary stances—
Remark how well I'm groomed,
I will explore your subtly-voiced nuances
Where delicacy is conscious but not false,
And take your hand, as if you were someone else.

Home forgotten, rediscover
Among chirruping of voices, chink of glass,
Those simple needs that turned us into lovers,
How solitary was the wilderness
Until we met, took leave of hosts and guests,
And with delicate consciousness of what was false
Walked off together, as if there were no one else.

Visiting Miss Emily

When you visit Aunt Em you must whistle
Through railings, and her face will glide
Like a slow white moon to the window-space.

Then you must wait patiently
By the bruised door—(put your ear
Against it, you will hear how slow she comes).

When it opens, say with unusual breeziness
How are you then? but don't listen
For an answer. Instead, go down

Stairs murky as a lost century
And emerge in her underground cavern
Where a cat will panic in the darkness.

There, make as much noise as you can—
Hum, whistle, scrape a chair—before
She enters with that curious and catching malady

Of never having been or done anything.
While you stay, be on your guard.
She is a siren, although she weighs five stone

From some illness she has never recovered from,
Although her hair is thin and lank as a washing-up rag,
Although she keeps a finger crooked to stop a ring falling
off.

Soon she will be capering for you, telling stories
of how during the war she'd dive under the bed
So that the falling bomb would bounce back from the
    springs;

Of how the sole stripped from her shoe, and she walked
A mile sliding her foot to stop the cod's-mouth flap—
She flickers to life with visits; she forgets,

And soon you'll be groaning and wheezing, helpless.
But keep your wits about you; remember she
Is your kin. Haven't you seen somewhere

That paleness of eyes? that pallor of cheeks?
Haven't you known what it is to slump like that?
Isn't this cavern familiar? and the filtered daylight?

Wish her goodbye. Kiss her cheek as if it were lovely.
Thank her for the soft biscuits and the rancid butter.
Then straighten your tie, pull your cuffs square,

Think of tomorrow as a day when the real begins
With its time and teabreaks. Tell her you'll
Visit her again sometime, one quiet Sunday.

'I Know She Sleeps'

I know she sleeps, in the room above me
a mind has suddenly ceased to prowl.
And farther off two children sleep
with the primal quick breast-heavings of
stoat or fox. Their sheets are warm as leaves.

I know she sleeps, for the silence comes
immediate, a thumbing of a switch,
a circuit breaking by which I am complete.
And this lamp holds what is left of light and warmth
and my fingers on this page are the remnant shapers

as silence dismantles the house. I would recall
all I have seen today—the adjacent falsehoods,
the grotesque distance sucked close on a screen,
one face turned generously towards me. I would assert
public disgrace, and the primacy of love,

but I only see the ink impress
a silent wilderness with words as scant
as bird-tracks in the snow—thin
hieroglyphs of presence, tokens of
a single skirmish in a hungry place.

BRIAN PATTEN

ROBERT NYE

JEREMY ROBSON

HUGO WILLIAMS

JON STALLWORTHY

ANGELA LANGFIELD

b. 1943. At present doing post-graduate work in philosophy at University College, London. Her poems have been published by the *Northwest Review* (USA), *Tribune*, *Poesie Vivante* and in the *Without Adam* anthology.

Living With You

There's a knack in living with you.
I don't have it.

There's a certain rhythm.
I'm out of time.

There's a skill
in talking you round,
adjusting the balance,
keeping it level, yet
with me it swings down.

There's an art
in letting you have your own way,
without knowing it;
always on the winning side
always king of the castle.

There must be a way
of loving you—
giving you everything,
still getting free.

Yet every time I am caught,
every time waved down,
and taken for questioning.

Car

This neatly packed up scrap iron heap,
thrown out roof and wings alight,
is his chariot, making a good death—
a restrained burning, like a fire kindled
in some private grate.

The side of the road
is a civilised place to die.

It did it very well, quietly, without a fuss,
as if the running stream of molten car
knew its audience.

The driver watched it go without a word.
He would have flapped
with shut off engines
into the middle of the road,
gone to pieces noisily,
trailing the flames that grew out of him
like hair, suddenly unclasped, fanned out
to make a better show,
a more spectacular end,
a more memorable death.

Reclining Figure
(Henry Moore)

I like you lying there
like something the sea washed up,
cat brought in or
man left on bed, clumsy on
the way out to work.

I like you lying
shamble of breasts and holes,
part of a car smash,
part of a love match, a
remnant of moulded sheets,
pockets of air in your legs.

I like you
when sideways a relief map, in
front Stonehenge, and now
close to, a monster, then
thumb marks make
nonsense of a lump of stone
touched quickly; hunched up rear.

MICHAEL LONGLEY

b. 1939 and brought up in Belfast. He was educated at the
Royal Belfast Academical Institution and at Trinity College,
Dublin. He has taught in Dublin, London and Belfast, and is
at present employed by the Arts Council of Northern Ireland
as its Literature Officer. He was poetry critic for the *Irish Times*
for several years, and has also written on painting and jazz. He
has published various pamphlets and one book of poems, *No
Continuing City* (1969). He is married and has a daughter.

In Memoriam

My father, let no similes eclipse
Where crosses like some forest simplified
Sink roots into my mind, the slow sands
Of history delay till through your eyes
I read you like a book. Before you died,
Re-enlisting with all the broken soldiers
You bent beneath your rucksack, near collapse,
In anecdote rehearsed and summarised
These words I write in memory. Let yours
And other heartbreaks play into my hands.

Now I see in close-up, in my mind's eye,
The cracked and splintered dead for pity's sake
Each dismal evening predecease the sun,
You, looking death and nightmare in the face
With your kilt, harmonica and gun,
Grow older in a flash, but none the wiser
(Who, following the wrong queue at The Palace,
Have joined the London Scottish by mistake),
Your nineteen years uncertain if and why
Belgium put the kibosh on the Kaiser.

Between the corpses and the soup canteens
You swooned away, watching your future spill.
But, as it was, your proper funeral urn
Had mercifully smashed to smithereens,
To shrapnel shards that sliced your testicle.

That instant I, your most unlikely son,
In No Man's Land was surely left for dead,
Blotted out from your far horizon.
As your voice now is locked inside my head,
I yet was held secure, waiting my turn.

Finally, that lousy war was over.
Stranded in France and in need of proof
You hunted down experimental lovers,
Persuading chorus girls and countesses:
This, father, the last confidence you spoke.
In my twentieth year your old wounds woke
As cancer. Lodging under the same roof
Death was a visitor who hung about,
strewing the house with pills and bandages,
Till he chose to put your spirit out.

Though they overslept the sequence of events
Which ended with the ambulance outside,
You lingering in the hall, your bowels on fire,
Tears in your eyes, and all your medals spent,
I summon girls who packed at last and went
Underground with you. Their souls again on hire,
Now those lost wives as recreated brides
Take shape before me, materialise.
On the verge of light and happy legend
They lift their skirts like blinds across your eyes.

Elegy for Fats Waller

Lighting up, lest all our hearts should break,
His fiftieth cigarette of the day,
Happy with so many notes at his beck
And call, he sits there taking it away,
The maker of immaculate slapstick.

With music and with such precise rampage
Across the deserts of the blues a trail
He blazes, towards the one true mirage,
Enormous on a nimble-footed camel
And almost refusing to be his age.

He plays for hours on end and though there be
Oases one part water, two parts gin,
He tumbles past to reign, wise and thirsty,
At the still centre of his loud dominion—
THE SHOOK THE SHAKE THE SHEIKH OF ARABY.

Circe

The cries of the shipwrecked enter my head.
On wildest nights when the torn sky confides
Its face to the sea's cracked mirror, my bed
—Addressed by the moon and her tutored brides—

Through brainstorm, through nightmare and ocean
Keeps me afloat. Shallows are my coven,
The comfortable margins—in this notion
I stand uncorrected by the sun even.

Out of the night husband after husband
—Eyes wide as oysters, arms full of driftwood—
Wades ashore and puts in at my island.
My necklaces of sea shells and sea weed,

My skirts of spindrift, sandals of flotsam
Catch the eye of each bridegroom for ever.
Quite forgetful of the widowing calm
My sailors wait through bad and good weather.

At first in rock pools I became their wife,
Under the dunes at last they lie with me—
These are the spring and neap tides of their life.
I have helped so many sailors off the sea,

And, counting no man among my losses,
I have made of my arms and my thighs last rooms
For the irretrievable and capsized—
I extend the sea, its idioms.

Journey Out of Essex

(or, John Clare's Escape from the Madhouse)

I am lying with my head
Over the edge of the world,
Unpicking my whereabouts
Like the asylum's name
That they stitch on the sheets.

Sick now with bad weather
Or a virus from the fens,
I dissolve in a puddle
My biographies of birds
And the names of flowers.

That they may recuperate
Alongside the stunned mouse,
The hedgehog rolled in leaves,
I am putting to bed
In this rheumatic ditch

The boughs of my harvest-home,
My wives, one on either side,
And keeping my head low as
A lark's nest, my feet toward
Helpston and the pole star.

DEREK MAHON

b. 1941 in Northern Ireland and educated at the Royal Belfast
Academical Institution and Trinity College, Dublin, where he
read Modern Languages. He has lived and worked in Dublin,
Belfast, London, the United States and Canada, and has had
various jobs which include warehouseman, Xerox operator,
barman, teacher and lecturer. He is now living in London.
His first full collection of poems, *Night Crossing*, published in
1968, was the Poetry Book Society Choice. He is a founder-
editor of the quarterly, *Ariel*.

In Belfast

Walking among my own this windy morning
In a tide of sunlight between shower and shower,
I resume my old conspiracy with the wet
Stone and the unwieldy images of the squinting heart.
Once more, as before, I remember not to forget.

There is a perverse pride in being on the side
Of the fallen angels and refusing to get up.
We could *all* be saved by keeping an eye on the hill
At the top of every street, for there it is—
Eternally, if irrelevantly, visible—

But yield instead to the humorous formulae,
The spurious mystery in the knowing nod.
Or we keep sullen silence in light and shade,
Rehearsing our astute salvations under
The cold gaze of a sanctimonious God.

One part of my mind must learn to know its place—
The things that happen in the kitchen-houses
And echoing back-streets of this desperate city
Should engage more than my casual interest,
Exact more interest than my casual pity.

My Wicked Uncle

It was my first funeral.
Some loss of status as a nephew since
Dictates that I recall
My numbness, my grandfather's hesitance,
My five aunts busy in the hall.

I found him closeted with living souls—
Coffined to perfection in the bedroom.
Death had deprived him of his moustache,
His thick horn-rimmed spectacles,
The easy corners of his salesman dash
(Those things by which I had remembered him)
And sundered him behind unnatural gauze.
His hair was badly parted on the right
As if for Sunday school. That night
I saw my uncle as he really was.

The narrative he dispensed was mostly
Wicked avuncular fantasy—
He went in for waistcoats and haircream.
But something about him
Demanded that you picture the surprise
Of the chairman of the board, when to
'What will you have with your whisky?' my uncle replies—
'Another whisky please'.

Once he was jailed in New York
Twice on the same day—
The crookedest chief steward in the Head Line.
And once (he affected communism)
He brought the whole crew out on strike
In protest at the loss of a day's pay
Crossing the international date line.

They buried him slowly above the sea,
The young Presbyterian Minister
Rumpled and windy in the sea air.
A most absorbing ceremony—
Ashes to ashes, dust to dust.
I saw sheep huddled in the long wet grass
Of the golf-course, and the empty freighters
Sailing for ever down Belfast Lough
In the fine rain, their sirens going,
As the gradual graph of my uncle's life and
Times dipped precipitately
Into the bowels of Carnmoney Cemetery.

His teenage kids are growing horns and claws—
More wicked already than ever my uncle was.

Jail Journal

For several days I have been under
House-arrest. My table has become
A sundial to its empty bottle.
With wise abandon
Lover and friend have gone.

In the window opposite
An old lady sits each afternoon
Talking to no one. I shout.
Either she is deaf or
She has reason.

I have books, provisions, running water
And a little stove. It would not matter
If cars moved silently at night
And no light or laughter
Came from the houses down the street.

It is taking longer than almost anything—
But I know, when it is over
And back come friend and lover,
I shall forget it like a childhood illness
Or a sleepless night-crossing.

Day Trip to Donegal

For Paul Smyth

We reached the sea in early afternoon,
Climbed stiffly out. There were urgent things to be done—
Clothes to be picked up, people to be seen.
As ever, the near-by hills were a deeper green
Than anywhere in the world, and the grave
Grey of the sea the grimmer in that enclave.

Down at the pier the boats gave up their catch—
Torn mouths and spewed-up lungs. They fetch
Ten times as much in the city as there,
And still the fish comé in year after year—
Herring and whiting, flopping about the deck
In attitudes of agony and heartbreak.

How could we hope to make them understand?
Theirs is a sea-mind, mindless upon land
And dead. Their systematic genocide
(Nothing remarkable that millions died)
To us is a necessity
For ours are land-minds, mindless in the sea.

We left at eight, drove back the way we came,
The sea receding down each muddy lane.
Around midnight we changed-down into suburbs
Sunk in a sleep no gale-force wind disturbs.
The time of year had left its mark
On frosty pavements glistening in the dark.

Give me a ring, goodnight, and so to bed . . .
That night the slow sea washed against my head,
Performing its immeasurable erosions—
Spilling into the skull, marbling the stones
That spine the very harbour wall,
Uttering its threat to villages of landfall.

At dawn I was alone far out at sea
Without skill or reassurance (nobody
To show me how, no earnest of rescue),
Cursing my mindless failure to take due
Forethought for this, contriving vain
Overtures to the mindless wind and rain.

Ecclesiastes

God, you could grow to love it, God-fearing, God-
    chosen purist little puritan that,
for all your wiles and smiles, you are (the
    dank churches, the empty streets,
the shipyard silence, the tied-up swings) and
    shelter your cold heart from the heat
of the world, from woman-inquisition, from the
    bright eyes of children. Yes, you could
wear black, drink water, nourish a fierce zeal
    with locusts and wild honey and not
feel called upon to understand and forgive
    but only to speak with a bleak
afflatus, and love the January rains when they
    darken the dark doors and sink hard
into the Antrim hills, the bog meadows, the heaped
    graves of your fathers. Bury that red
bandanna and stick, that banjo; this is your
    country, close one eye and be king.
Your people await you, their heavy washing
    flaps for you in the housing estates—
a credulous people. God, you could do it, God
    help you, stand on a corner stiff
with rhetoric, promising nothing under the sun.

H

DOM MORAES

b. India 1939. Has lived mainly in London since graduating from Oxford University in 1959. He has published three books of poems; *A Beginning* (1957), which won the Hawthornden Prize, *Poems* (1960) and *John Nobody* (1965). His *Selected Poems* appeared in America in 1966. Apart from this he is represented in *Penguin Modern Poets, 2*, has written an autobiographical book, *My Son's Father*, and a travel book entitled *Gone Away*.

Gone Away

My native city rose from sea,
Its littered frontiers wet and dark.
Time came too soon to disembark
And rain like buckshot sprayed my head.
My dreams, I thought, lacked dignity.
So I got drunk and went to bed.

But dreamt of you all night, and felt
More lonely at the break of day
And trod, to brush the dream away,
The misted pavements where rain fell.
There the consumptive beggars knelt,
Voiced with the thin voice of a shell.

The records that those pavements keep,
Bronze relics from the beggar's lung,
Oppress me, fastening my tongue.
Seawhisper in the rocky bay
Derides me, and when I find sleep,
The parakeets shriek that away.

Except in you I have no rest,
For always with you I am safe:
Who now am far, and mime the deaf
Though you call gently as a dove.
Yet each day turns to wander west:
And every journey ends in love.

At Seven O'Clock

The masseur from Ceylon, whose balding head
Gives him a curious look of tenderness,
Uncurls his long crushed hands above my bed
As though he were about to preach or bless.

His poulterer's fingers pluck my queasy skin,
Shuffle along my side, and reach the thigh.
I note however that he keeps his thin
Fastidious nostrils safely turned away.

But sometimes the antarctic eyes glance down,
And the lids drop to hood a scornful flash:
A deep ironic knowledge of the thin
Or gross (but always ugly) human flesh.

Hernia, goitre and the flowering boil
Lie bare beneath his hands, for ever bare.
His fingers touch the skin: they reach the soul.
I know him in the morning for a seer.

Within my mind he is reborn as Christ:
For each blind dawn he kneads my prostrate thighs,
Thumps on my buttocks with his fist
And breathes, Arise.

War Correspondent

At dusk I drove back to the painted city
Through tawny dunes feathered with tamarisk.
Alex still filled the bar, tirelessly witty,
Keeping the flies off with a native whisk
    Plied without pity.

He welcomed me in his effusive way.
The white dust in my hair gave me a look,
Alex said affably, *très distingué*.
He had relaxed, he added, with a book,
    During the day.

My hundred miles of dust called for a shower.
I came back to observe once more how Alex,
When dipped in whisky, opened like a flower.
He told me then that unrest in the barracks
    Spread hour by hour.

He said this was the fault of the dictator
And said dictators were no friends to life.
Alex had had experience in the matter.
Horthy he named, and Franco, and his wife.
    A little later.

But while dictators have whole lands to kill
We only had tonight—dictators spoiled
Nightlife, he said—but there were places still.
The manager, his brown eyes newly oiled,
    Bowed with the bill.

Outside, like large doors slammed a long way off,
Enemy cannon thudded in the sky.
'Do shut up' Alex told them, 'that's enough',
And hummed in a morose and stumbling way,
    'Let there be love'.

His pale face with its red aureole of hair
Looked suddenly so bored that it seemed dead.
'I don't know *why* it is that everywhere's
So boring. But there *is* a place', he said.
    'Shall we try there?'

Rendezvous★

Altermann, sipping wine, reads with a look
Of infinite patience and slight suffering.
When I approach him, he puts down his book,

Waves to the chair beside him like a king,
Then claps his hands, and an awed waiter fetches
Bread, kosher sausage, cake, a chicken's wing,

More wine, some English cigarettes, and matches.
'Eat, eat', Altermann says, 'this is good food'.
Through the awning over us the sunlight catches

His aquiline sad head, till it seems hewed
From tombstone marble. I accept some bread.
I've lunched already, but would not seem rude.

When I refuse more, he feeds me instead,
Heaping my plate, clapping for wine, his eyes
—Expressionless inside the marble head—

Appearing not to notice how the flies
Form a black, sticky icing on the cake.
Thinking of my health now, I visualise

★ Part 1 of a sequence of 'Two Poems from Israel'

The Aryan snow floating, flake upon flake,
Over the ghetto wall where only fleas
Fed well, and they and hunger kept awake

Under sharp stars, those waiting for release.
Birds had their nests, but Jews nowhere to hide
When visited by vans and black police.

The shekinah rose where a people died,
A pillar of flame by night, of smoke by day.
From Europe then the starved and terrified

Flew. Now their mourner sits in this café,
Telling me how to scan a Hebrew line.
Though my attention has moved far away

His features stay marble and aquiline.
But the eternal gesture of his race
Flowing through the hands that offer bread and wine

Reveals the deep love sealed in the still face.

Snow on a Mountain

That dream, her eyes like rocks studded the high
Mountain of her body that I was to climb.
    One moment past my hands had swum
    The chanting streams of her thighs:
Then I was lost, breathless among the pines.

Alone, alone with the nervous noise of water,
Climbing, I hoped to emerge on a path, but I knew
    When the spurred trees were past
    I should go on no further
But fall there, dazzled by the miles of snow.

My dream was broken by the knock of day.
Yet, within my mind, these pictures linger:
    I touch her with my clumsy words of love
    And sense snow in her eye,
Mists, and the winds that warn, Stranger, O stranger!

ROBERT NYE

b. London 1939. His formal education in state schools ended at the age of sixteen, at which time his first poems were published in *The London Magazine*. He has been a professional writer ever since, subsidising his own creative writing by a good deal of literary, critical and journalistic activity. He has published three books of poems: *Juvenilia 1* (1961), *Juvenilia 2* (1963) and *Darker Ends* (1969). His other publications include a novel, *Doubtfire* (1968), a volume of short stories *Tales I Told My Mother* (1969) and several books for children. He has also written plays for stage and radio and edited selections from Ralegh and Swinburne. He lives in Edinburgh, is married and has six children.

Darker Ends

Here's my hand turned to shadows on the wall—
Black horse, black talking fox, black crocodile—
Quick fingers beckoning darkness from white flame,
Until my son screams, 'No! chase them away!'

Why do I scare him? Fearful of my love
I'm cruelly comforted by his warm fear,
Seeing the night made perfect on the wall
In my handwriting, if illegible,
Still full of personal beasts, and terrible.

Abjure that art—it is no true delight
To lie and turn the dark to darker ends
Because my heart's dissatisfied and cold.
To tell the truth, when he is safe asleep,
I shut my eyes and let the darkness in.

An Absence of Nettles

I like nettles, but I took
the cold scythe for your sake
To clean the way where you would walk
And make it possible
For your foreshadowed flowers.

An evening I worked there,
And another, longer; gripping
The ancient handles with a clumsy craft,
Swinging the rusty blade about my knees,
Crouched to listen to it.

The keen heads of nettles
Lopped without pity
Were raked and carried up
To a black-hearted bonfire;
The shaven earth was ready.

I pulled up such roots
As the hands can find,
And cast away pebbles;
Weeding and watering
My own grave.

But now—no flowers have come
To fit your shadows;
The earth will not accept
The seeds you sow. And who can care for
An absence of nettles, an ungrowing place?

Crowson

He died at the proper time, on Christmas Day
As we sat down to dinner—an old man
With no friends and no vices, blindly mean
With the kind of love that goes with being clean,
His chief possessions a sour bar of soap,
A flannel which reeked of him, and a steel comb
He used to keep his dry grey hair in order
Over the face as hard and proud as a doorknob;
A sick old man, but acting out his illness,
A broken man, but whole and straight in cunning,
A man whom no one loved or liked or pitied,
Whom we had wished would die, for the work's sake.
And yet, I think, I did not wish him harm.

Well he was dead at last, on Christmas Day,
And spoiled our dinner. 'Just like him', said Twitch,
'To go and die now, after seven months
Of not quite dying. Just like him to save
His death for the wrong time, when no one's ready.
Who wants to lay out a corpse on Christmas Day?
It would serve him right if we left him, eh?'
And I agreed (although I was dismayed
Not to feel much beyond an amateur
Distaste for death) nodding in a paper crown,
Grinning at brother Twitch across a table
Set out with crackers, beer, cheap cigarettes.

Dinner completed and our bellies full,
Half-cut we went to Crowson's room.
He lay, the oxygen mask ridiculously sucked
Into his blue mouth, fish-eyes mocking us.
Beside the neat bed, on the locker,
His watch ticked fussily; his corpse
Scarcely disturbed the counterpane's perfection,

So thin he had become in these last days.
Twitch belched. 'We'd better get him over with.'

And then Twitch bullied
That sticky carcass, punched it here and there
About the bed, about the usual business:
A bag of bones shoved rudely in death's costume.
He mocked the stale flesh, fey in this last gesture—
'A Christmas present, darling'—tying a bow
On the penis, where a knot would have done,
Flirting with the shroud
As if it were the dress of some gay girl,
Taking revenge for all the dead one's age
And ugliness, knowing he would come
To this too soon—and, most of all,
For spoiling our Christmas dinner.

This is no elegy, for I did not love you,
Crowson, old man smelling of soap and tuberculosis;
Surely, for all my wrong, I did not love you
As queer Twitch did, who used you then so cruelly.
And yet, I think, I did not wish you harm.
Am I to blame for what he did to you?
The question in its asking answers 'Yes':
For where did Twitch begin and such fear end
As made me cold, incapable of tears
Or useful rage till this? and in these words
Which cannot warm you now, nor yet avenge
The insult you did not feel in my name,
The bullying no buffet could atone,
Nor prayer nor haunting expiate.

It was my faint white heart which hit you there.
It was my greed of self deflowered you
And bruised you in your death, which you thought
    perfect.

To ask forgiveness were another insult—
I will ask nothing but that you forget
You ever knew me, as I would forget
The big day I was born, keeping in mind
The day you died. I am forgetting now
In hope I will remember you more clearly
And in your memory wish no harm more dearly.

In More's Hotel

(for Aileen)

Wasn't it just that
we touched for the first time
the mother string
the pearls are threaded on?

Or was it especially
a key, a bible—
a litany of chance
which found again
would spell us close
as we were then
in More's hotel,
learning our alphabet.

Last night it was cloud
against the pane, twice
you dreamt it.
This morning I turn on a tap and water
is water alone, relating
to keys and bibles
by a cordial difference,
not very likely, but all the same
married and holding together well.

BRIAN PATTEN

b. Liverpool 1946 and educated at a local secondary modern school. He has done a great many poetry readings throughout the country and published two books of poems, *Little Johnny's Confession* (1967) and *Notes to the Hurrying Man* (1969). He appears in the *Liverpool Scene* anthology and in *Penguin Modern Poets, 10*. He has also written a children's story, *The Adventures of Nathan and Xemeplonk*. He now lives in London.

Little Johnny's Final Letter

Mother,

> I won't be home this evening, so
> don't worry; don't hurry to report me missing.
> Don't drain the canals to find me,
> I've decided to stay alive, don't
> search the woods, I'm not hiding,
> simply gone to get myself classified.
> Don't leave my shreddies out,
> I've done with security.
> Don't circulate my photograph to society
> I have disguised myself as a man
> and am giving priority to obscurity.
> It suits me fine:
> I have taken off my short trousers
> and put on long ones, and
> now am going out into the city, so
> don't worry; don't hurry to report me missing.
>
> I've rented a room without any curtains
> and sit behind the windows growing cold,
> heard your plea on the radio this morning,
> you sounded sad and strangely old. . . .

Ode on Celestial Music

(or: *It's The Girl In The Bathroom Singing*)

It's not celestial music it's the girl in the bathroom singing.
You can tell. Although it's winter
the trees outside her window have grown leaves,
all manner of flowers push up through the floorboards.
I think—what a filthy trick that is to play on me,
I snip them with my scissors shouting
'*I want only bona fide celestial music!*'
Hearing this she stops singing.

Out of her bath now the girl knocks on my door,
'Is my singing disturbing you?' she smiles entering,
'did you say it was licentious or sensual?
And excuse me, my bath towel's slipping.'
A warm and blonde creature
I slam the door on her breasts shouting
'*I want only bona fide celestial music!*'

Much later on in life I wear my hearing-aid.
What have I done to my body, ignoring it,
splitting things into so many pieces my hands
cannot mend anything. The stars, the buggers, remained
    silent.
Down in the bathroom now her daughter is singing.
Turning my hearing-aid full volume
I bend close to the floorboards hoping
for at least one flower to appear.

You Come to Me Quiet as Rain Not Yet Fallen

You come to me quiet as rain not yet fallen
afraid of how you might fail yourself your
dress seven summers old is kept open
in memory of sex, smells warm, of boys,
and of the once long grass.
But we are colder now; we have not
love's first magic here. You come to me
quiet as bulbs not yet broken
out into sunlight.

The fear I see in your now lining face
changes to puzzlement when my hands reach
for you as branches reach. Your dress
does not fall easily, nor does your body
sing of its own accord. What love added to
a common shape no longer seems a miracle.
You come to me with your age wrapped in excuses
and afraid of its silence.

Into the paradise our younger lives made
of this bed and room
has leaked the world and all its questioning
and now those shapes terrify most
that remind us of our own. Harder now
to check longings or sentiment, to care overmuch,
you look out across years, come to me
quiet as the last of our senses closing.

JEREMY ROBSON

b. 1939. He is the regular poetry reviewer for *Tribune*, and has written criticism for a number of magazines including *Encounter* and *Twentieth Century*. He is editor of the anthology of *Poems from Poetry and Jazz in Concert* and originator of the programmes from which these were taken. He has published two books of poems, *Thirty-Three Poems* (1964) and *In Focus* (1970). He lives in London and is chief editor of the publishers, Vallentine, Mitchell.

Words to a Conductor

(for David Atherton)

I

The notes are there to start
though the art you give to them
brings pulse-beat, texture, voice
where silence was: the voice
admittedly not yours, but not

his either, quite, who wrote
them down. Your energies involve
themselves at will: tensions, doubts
compound. Last night's row, this
morning's tiff, the dash through

traffic in failing light, a
shirt too stiff, bow too tight—
all crowd, line up for the attack,
are stifled by the disciplines imposed
yet show. Words work less liberally.

Write 'black', the speaker's voice
says 'black'. You have a colour and
a social cause, Othello, riots, cool
Chicago jazz, must choose. Besides,
before you lift your pen you've scanned

the morning mail, stared headlines
out, answered four calls, switched on
switched off the news, a man from the
Electricity Board has called, you've
traded words, are bored, go out.

II

Hard hours later, and our set's
ablaze. You're 'live' from the Albert
Hall, and the announcer's giving way.
Above the instruments' tense scrawl
a vibrant hush is rising to applause.

Outside snow drifts mysteriously;
a tree, raped of its branches,
stares vulnerably back, deposed.
The journey home today by British
Rail has been a babbling Hell

everything means something else.
The Overture breaks through, my tree
takes wings; the snow is somewhere
vast, Siberia perhaps, unrolls.
To tie this with a language that's exact

that *means*, is tone, is colour, shape
is all the things that you and painters
talk about, and more, is what we
try, and still you wonder why
there's 'nothing new' this week.

I envy you your abstract world, and all
that's caught in the music's swell:
a tempest or a nuclear war,
Napoleon's campaigns, a reveller's
sigh, pauper's curse, patron's snore

all there, or less, or more,
removed from the dictionary's stare,
the word worn thin by use, islanded,
abused, there on its own terms, refined
undefined, a baton's beat away.

Waking

Waking, you said you saw your house,
the Nile snaking into mist,
Mohammed the one-eyed cook.
Somehow, you said, there were children,
running . . .

And I have watched you waking,
breaking from an Orient
half-hinted at in gestures, frowns
a craze for things with spice,
pepper, pomegranate, pimento, rice,
love of the desert, rock, the open sky.

And in you, grave refugee,
I catch an ancient plight:
not crammed in trucks
not stoned on sight
hounded by Inquisition
or crusading zeal,
but turned
without word without sound
from shore to sea: Suez, '56—
a Cairo-born French-speaking
Spanish Jewess on the wing.

It was wonderful, marvellous, you say
the late sun thumbing the Nile
the children running . . .
And away you go into dream:
the new London day dismissed
the four safe walls,
the friend that guards, regards you,
comes so close, retreats,
hearing a voice troubled in sleep
calling a new name, in a strange tongue,
distant and complete.

Reflection in Winter

Sick of it all, the whole persona: the smile
snapped to tame lips at his master's call,
lingering too long: the head nodding Yes
when the head thinks No: the issues let
drop, shrugged off, not worth the candle:
the whole damned manner too mild by far, a lie
masking a force coiled to breaking point.

Sick of being here, there, of the season's
fickle mood, of today's speech, tomorrow's
march, of the drizzle in the amber lights—
and most of all, sick of you my friend
yes YOU
your reflection there, cock-a-hoop,
smug in the store's dusty glass,
another cut-price bargain for men!
I shut my eyes: you're gone.
I turn: you're back the other side.

One day, I swear, I'll do it, unleash it all,
my umbrella raised just so—and
smash! handle first through the nearest
pane I catch you sniggering from.
Imagine the fuss, the salesman's stark face,
the Piccadilly traffic spun to a halt.
And imagine *her* face, caught
so off-guard, so credulous.

And in court, the friends lined up
to defend the man they knew.
Your worship, truly, just a lapse,
a black moment, an urge, you mustn't think,
not for one moment . . .

No! Not for a moment.
Not of the noise, the pandemonium, glass
showered like confetti on this year's suit.
You'd only turn away, as now,
shrug it slowly off,
smile.

Untouchables

The ones that get away
are the ones that stick,
catch in the throat like bones,
return to haunt and leer.

Often they are ordinary,
encounters on tubes or buses,
angry exchanges when the quips
arrived too lame, leaving me
to froth at mirrors, hopelessly.
Words, words, falling too slow
or too quick, ridiculous!

Or those in need of help,
the blind man injured in a street
because I moved too late, just
too late, too hesitantly. . . .
Catches dropped, goals missed,
the timeless catalogue.

And women by the score,
plump women and slim women,
untouchables from cocktail parties,
the too-talls and the too-poised,
so often and so many

parading past like whores,
their breasts loose, their
buttocks swaying freakishly,
on, through my dreams,
through the reeling mind,
down the shafts of sleep.

JON STALLWORTHY

b. 1935 and educated at Rugby and Magdalen College, Oxford, where he won the Newdigate prize for poetry in 1958, having been runner-up in 1957. For three years (on and off) he represented the University at rugby football, but never got a 'blue'. He has worked as an editor with the Oxford University Press for ten years. His publications include three books of poems, *The Astronomy of Love* (1961), *Out of Bounds* (1963) and *Root and Branch* (1969), two books on Yeats and translations of Alexander Blok. He co-edited the 1970 PEN anthology.

No Ordinary Sunday

No ordinary Sunday. First the light
Falling dead through dormitory windows blind
With fog; and then, at breakfast, every plate
Stained with the small, red cotton flower; and no
Sixpence for pocketmoney. Greatcoats, lined
By the right, marched from their pegs, with slow
Poppy fires smouldering in one lapel
To light us through the fallen cloud. Behind
That handkerchief sobbed the quick Sunday bell.

A granite cross, the school field underfoot,
Inaudible prayers, hymn-sheets that stirred
Too loudly in the hand. When hymns ran out,
Silence, like silt, lay round so wide and deep
It seemed that winter held its breath. We heard
Only the river talking in its sleep:
Until the bugler flexed his lips, and sound
Cutting the fog cleanly like a bird,
Circled and sang out over the bandaged ground.

Then low voiced, the headmaster called the roll
of those who could not answer; every name
Suffixed with honour—'double first', 'kept goal
For Cambridge'—and a death—in spitfires, tanks,
And ships torpedoed. At his call there came
Through the mist blond heroes in broad ranks
With rainbows struggling on their chests. Ahead
Of us, in strict step, as we idled home
Marched the formations of the towering dead.

November again, and the bugles blown
In a tropical Holy Trinity,
The heroes today stand further off, grown
Smaller but distinct. They flash no medals, keep
No ranks: through *Last Post* and *Reveille*
Their chins loll on their chests, like birds asleep.
Only when the long, last note ascends
Upon the wings of kites, some two or three
Look up and have the faces of my friends.

A Letter from Berlin

My dear,
               Today a letter from Berlin
where snow—the first of '38—flew in,
settled and shrivelled on the lamp last night,
broke moth wings mobbing the window. Light
woke me early, but the trams were late:
I had to run from the Brandenburg Gate
skidding, groaning like a tram, and sodden
to the knees. Von Neumann operates at 10
and would do if the sky fell in. They lock
his theatre doors on the stroke of the clock—
but today I was lucky: found a gap
in the gallery next to a chap
I knew just as the doors were closing. Last,
as expected, on Von Showman's list
the new vaginal hysterectomy
that brought me to Berlin.

Delicately
he went to work, making from right to left
a semi-circular incision. Deft
dissection of the fascia. The blood-
blossoming arteries nipped in the bud.
Speculum, scissors, clamps—the uterus
cleanly delivered, the pouch of Douglas
stripped to the rectum, and the cavity
closed. Never have I seen such masterly
technique. 'And so little bleeding!' I said
half to myself, half to my neighbour.

'Dead',
came his whisper. 'Don't be a fool'
I said, for still below us in the pool
of light the marvellous unhurried hands
were stitching, tying the double strands
of catgut, stitching, tying. It was like
a concert, watching those hands unlock
the music from their score. And at the end
one half expected him to turn and bend
stiffly towards us. Stiffly he walked out
and his audience shuffled after. But
finishing my notes in the gallery
I saw them uncover the patient: she
was dead.

I met my neighbour in the street
waiting for the same tram, stamping his feet
on the pavement's broken snow, and said
'I have to apologise. She was dead,
but how did you know?' Back came his voice
like a bullet '—saw it last month, twice'.

Returning your letter to an envelope
yellower by years than when you sealed it up,
darkly the omens emerge. A ritual wound
yellow at the lip yawns in my hand;
a turbulent crater; a trench, filled
not with snow only, east of Buchenwald.

On The Road

The red lights running my way
keep their distance, hold their fire; the white
blaze from both barrels as they
lunge past. Headlamp and tail-light

switch in the mirror, white to red,
red to white as gears shift down
to overtake. Shot through the head
with lights I sway from town to town.

Red corpuscles, white corpuscles,
thread the branched arteries.
Cramp gnaws my anklebone, worries
the calf-muscle

wired to a pedal. Untuned now
the athlete's pulse stumbles through fat
that once ran steady as the flow
of petrol under my foot.

K

Cylinders leaping at the swerve
of the road inherit
our animal blood; I hear it
answer the summoning nerve

in other arteries. I have been
how many years on the road?
The dashboard reels off a ribbon
of figures I cannot read

for the ricochet of lights
from windscreen and wet street.
Long enough to remember nights
when blood through all its channels beat

with one current marrying white
and red. The sky over London
burns like my forehead; heat without
energy, light without vision.

Bacillae spawn in the bloodstream,
but the stream has outrun its poisons
before. I thread a fever-dream
of crossroads, straining to read the signs.

Two Hands

My father in his study sits up late,
a pencil nodding stiffly in the hand
that thirteen times between breakfast and
supper led a scalpel an intricate
dance. The phone has sobbed itself to sleep,

but he has articles to read. I curse
tonight, at the other end of the house,
this other hand whose indecisions keep
me cursing nightly; fingers with some style
on paper, elsewhere none. Who would have thought
hands so alike—spade palms, blunt fingers short
in the joint—would have no more in common? All
today, remembering the one, I have watched
the other save no one, serve no one, dance
with this pencil. Hand, you may have your chance
to stitch a life for fingers that have stitched
new life for many. Down the *Lancet* margin
his hand moves rapidly as mine moves slow.
A spasm shakes the phone at his elbow.
The pencil drops: he will be out again.

An Evening Walk

Taking my evening walk
where flats like liners ride
at anchor on a dark
phosphorus-rippled tide
of traffic, ebbing, flowing,
I heard from a kiosk
a telephone ringing;
from an empty kiosk.

Its dark voice welling up
out of the earth or air
for a moment made me stop,
listen, and consider

whether to break in
on its animal grief.
I could imagine
torrents of relief,

anger, explanation—
'*Oh for God's sake*'—but I'd
troubles of my own,
and passed on the other side.
All the same I wondered,
with every step I took,
what I would have heard
lifting it from the hook.

As I was returning
after the pubs were shut,
I found the bulb still burning
in the kiosk, but
the dark voice from the dark
had done with ringing:
the phone was off the hook
like a hanged man swinging.

HUGO WILLIAMS

b. Windsor 1942 and educated at Eton. In 1963 and 1964 he travelled extensively through Asia, Australia and the Pacific, writing a number of the poems in his first collection, *Symptoms of Loss* (1965). He won the 1966 E. C. Gregory Award, and in 1970 published his second book of poems, *Sugar Daddy*. He is assistant editor of *The London Magazine*.

The Couple Upstairs

Shoes instead of slippers down the stairs,
She ran out with her clothes

And the front door banged and I saw her
Walking crookedly, like naked, to a car.

She was not always with him up there,
And yet they seemed inviolate, like us,
Our loves in sympathy. Her going

Thrills and frightens us. We come awake
And talk excitedly about ourselves, like guests.

Sugar Daddy

You do not look like me. I'm glad
England failed to colonise
Those black orchid eyes
With blue, the colour of sun-blindness.

Your eyes came straight to you
from your mother's Martinique
Great-grandmother. They look at me
Across this wide Atlantic

With an inborn feeling for my weaknesses.
Like loveletters, your little phoney grins
Come always just too late
To reward my passionate clowning.

I am here to be nice, clap hands, reflect
your tolerance. I know what I'm for.
When you come home fifteen years from now
Saying you've smashed my car,

I'll feel the same. I'm blood brother,
Sugar-Daddy, millionaire to you.
I want to buy you things.

I bought a garish humming top
And climbed into your pen like an ape
And pumped it till it screeched for you,
Hungry for thanks. Your lip

Trembled and you cried. You did not need
My sinister grenade, something
Pushed out of focus at you, swaying
Violently. You owned it anyway

And the whole world it came from.
It was then I knew
I could only take things from you from now on.

I was the White Hunter,
Bearing cheap mirrors for the Chief,
you saw the giving-look coagulate in my eyes
And panicked for the trees.

UFO *On the District Line*

I was on a train. I missed the station.
Chinese children were looking at my nose.

I looked at them, their faces round as soap,
And saw it hovering mothlike between us.

This was new to me. My nose is breezy,
Even musical, but was never airborne till now.

I smiled uneasily, but the oriental stare
Stopped short of me, focusing on the danger.

Eventually I got out, and my nose
Flew swiftly back upon my face.

There was a slight hiss and the train
Disappeared laughing over Asia.

Beginning to Go

I watch your complicated face
In a three-sided looking glass,

Intent on a radio serial
As you pile the subtle

Darkness of your hair, each morning
More fantastic. Last evening

After two bottles of beer
We almost spoke: your sister

Manufactures silk in Bangkok.
She gets about £2 a week

And it's no bloody good. Your own
Work here is harder to explain:

We laugh at almost the same thing,
Uncertain whom the joke is on

And I keep thinking of what
Might have been, if this and that

And how the curtain soon will fall
With a question still

Unanswered, so many things left
Vaguely incomplete. The rift

Is here already though we laugh
At it. And though I laugh

I feel the dried-up sadness
Of it, like age coming into my face.

Acknowledgements

For poems by Taner Baybars, to the author for 'The Long Visitors' and 'Little Paul's Moon Hut', to the Scorpion Press for 'Burglary' from *To Catch a Falling Man* (1963); for poems by Keith Bosley, to the author for 'Number 14', to Macmillan for 'The Old Postcards' and 'Wind at Midnight' from *The Possibility of Angels* (1969); for poems by Stewart Conn, to the author for 'Tremors', 'Family Visit', and 'Suicide', to Hutchinson for 'Todd' and 'Ferret' from *Stoats in the Sunlight* (1968); for poems by Kevin Crossley-Holland, to the author; for poems by Peter Dale, to the author for 'Gift of Words' and 'In Memory of a Hungarian Poet Murdered by the Nazis', to Macmillan for 'There Will be Shots During the Performance' from *The Storms* (1968) and for 'Just Visiting' from *Mortal Fire* (1970); for poems by Douglas Dunn, to the author for 'The Hunched' and 'After the War', to Faber & Faber for 'The Clothes Pit', 'A Removal from Terry Street,' and 'A Dream of Judgement' from *Terry Street* (1969); for poems by John Fuller, to the author for 'Scenario for a Walk-on Part', to Chatto and Windus for 'Song' from *Fairground Music* (1961) and for 'Pictures from a '48 De Soto' and 'Peasant Woman: Rhodes' from *The Tree That Walked* (1967); for poems by Ian Hamilton, to Faber & Faber for poems from *The Visit* (1970); for poems by Tony Harrison, to the author for 'Durham', to London Magazine Editions for 'Thomas Campey and the Copernican System', 'A Proper Caution' and 'The Nuptial Torches' from *The Loiners* (1970); for poems by Seamus Heaney, to the author for 'Shore Woman', to Faber & Faber for 'Follower' from *Death of a Naturalist* (1966) and for 'The Outlaw', 'The Peninsula' and 'The Given Note' from *Door into the Dark* (1969); for poems by Douglas Hill, to the author; for poems by Glyn Hughes, to Macmillan for poems from *Neighbours* (1970); for poems by A. C. Jacobs, to the author; for poems by Brian Jones, to Alan Ross Ltd for 'Local Custom', 'Husband to Wife; Party-Going', and 'Visiting Miss Emily' from *Poems* (1966) and for 'I Know She Sleeps' from *Interior* (1969); for poems by Angela Langfield, to the author; for poems by Michael

Longley, to Macmillan for poems from *No Continuing City* (1969); for poems by Derek Mahon, to the author for 'Ecclesiastes', to Oxford University Press for 'In Belfast', 'My Wicked Uncle', 'Jail Journal', and 'Day Trip to Donegal' from *Night Crossing* (1968); for poems by Dom Moraes, to John Johnson for 'Snow on a Mountain' and 'At Seven O'Clock' from *A Beginning* (Panton Press, 1957) and for 'War Correspondent' from *Poems 1955–65* (Macmillan & Co, New York, 1966), to Eyre & Spottiswoode for 'Gone' from *Poems* (1960) and for 'Rendezvous' from *John Nobody* (1965); for poems by Robert Nye, to the author for 'From More's Hotel', to Calder & Boyars for 'Darker Ends,' 'An Absence of Nettles' and 'Crowson' from *Darker Ends* (1969); for poems by Brian Patten, to Allen & Unwin for 'You Come to Me Quiet as Rain Not Yet Fallen' and 'Ode on Celestial Music' from *Notes to the Hurrying Man* (1969), and for 'Little Johnny's Final Letter' from *Little Johnny's Confession* (1967); for poems by Jeremy Robson, to the author and Allison & Busby for poems from *In Focus* (1970); for poems by Jon Stallworthy, to Oxford University Press for 'No Ordinary Sunday' from *Out of Bounds* (1963), and to Chatto & Windus for 'A Letter from Berlin', 'On the Road', 'Two Hands' and 'An Evening Walk' from *Root & Branch* (1969); for poems by Hugo Williams, to Oxford University Press for 'Beginning to Go', from *Symptoms of Loss* (1965) and for 'Sugar Daddy', 'UFO On the District Line' and 'The Couple Upstairs' from *Sugar Daddy* (1970).

Date Due